SANTA ANA PUBLIC LIBRARY

TUNNELS

BY CASS R. SANDAK

An Easy-Read Modern Wonders Book

Franklin Watts
New York / London / Toronto / Sydney
1984

Over: **a steam engine on a cogwheel railway chugs out of a tunnel in the Swiss Alps.**

For my father and forefathers

R.L. 3.9 Spache Revised Formula

Cover photograph courtesy of Frank Sloan

Photographs courtesy of: Swiss National Tourist Office: pp. 1, 4, 7 (top right), 26 (left); Shostal: pp. 6 (bottom left), 14, 17, 22 (top right), 26 (right), 28; Bureau of Reclamation: pp. 6 (bottom right), 16, 17 (top); The Bettmann Archive: pp. 7 (top left), 23, 25 (top left), 29 (left); Fred J. Maroon: p. 7 (bottom left); Bay Area Rapid Transit: pp. 7 (bottom right), 20, 25 (bottom right); Virginia Department of Conservation: p. 8 (top left); New Mexico State Economic Development/Tourism Department: p. 8 (top right); the author: pp. 9, 15 (left), 18 (bottom left), 22 (top left), 24, 25 (bottom left); Frank Sloan: p. 10; NASA: p. 13; Ewing Galloway: pp. 15 (right), 18 (bottom right), 21 (left and right), 27 (bottom right); Chesapeake Bay Bridge and Tunnel Authority: p. 22 (bottom); New Jersey Department of Conservation and Economic Development: p. 27 (left); United Press International: p. 29.

Diagrams by Jane Kendall

Library of Congress Cataloging in Publication Data

Sandak, Cass R.
Tunnels.

(An Easy-read modern wonders book)
Includes index.
Summary: An introduction to tunnels including their history, how they are made, various kinds of tunnels and their construction, and their uses.
1. Tunnels—Juvenile literature. 2. Tunneling—Juvenile literature. [1. Tunnels. 2. Tunneling]
I. Title. II. Series.
TA807.S26 1984 624.1'93 83-25994
ISBN 0-531-04712-1

6 5 4 3 2 1

Contents

Today's tunnels cut through mountainous regions of the world. They allow modern superhighways to reduce travel time by many hours. Here, an entrance to the St. Gotthard Tunnel in Switzerland.

Underground Passageways

From the time that people lived in caves, tunnels have held special interest. Dark passageways under the earth contain mystery, danger, and adventure.

Thrilling stories tell of daring escapes through tunnels. The sewer tunnels under the city of Paris have been the setting for many exciting stories. Bank robbers have dug underground in order to steal money. During World War II, soldiers dug tunnels to escape their enemies. And brave East Germans still dig tunnels to freedom under the Berlin Wall.

In the news we hear reports of mine workers being trapped underground for days. South African workers who dig for gold may have to tunnel through passages nearly 2½ miles (4 km) below the surface of the earth. But mines are not like most tunnels because they do not lead anywhere.

Perhaps every child who has ever dug in the dirt with a shovel has dreamed of digging a tunnel all the way through the earth to China.

What Is a Tunnel?

A tunnel is an underground passage. It is usually level. Most man-made tunnels are large enough for people or vehicles to move through them. Narrow shafts and pipes that pass through the ground are not large enough to be called tunnels.

Tunnels may be only a few feet in length or many miles long. They make shortcuts that can save hours of travel time.

Tunnels pass through mountains, under city buildings and streets, and even under rivers, lakes, or sections of the ocean.

Tunnels connect buildings and underground shopping malls. In some places tunnels are even being used for offices and storage space.

Tunnels are dug to mine coal and minerals from far under the ground. Some tunnels even make energy. Hydroelectric tunnels supply power to modern cities. Water flows down a passage to turn

Left: the entrance to a tunnel on the Pennsylvania Turnpike. *Right:* the inside of the Stillwater Tunnel in Utah. This tunnel is part of a project that carries water to make power.

turbines at the end of the tunnel. These turbines make electric power for homes and businesses.

Millions of people use the subway, railroad, and automobile tunnels of our modern transportation systems every day. A tunnel that carries water is called an **aqueduct.** Tunnels bring fresh water into our cities and carry waste water and sewage away to treatment plants. And in more and more places, tunnels hold the gas mains, telephone lines, and electric lines that make our modern way of life possible. Tunnels are part of daily life.

Left: this tunnel in Colorado was hollowed out of granite. It is used by the U.S. Government as a storage and work place. *Right:* a Swiss tunnel and road near completion.

Left: a tunnel passes *under* Egypt's Suez Canal. *Right:* a modern subway station tunnel in San Francisco.

Right: train tracks pass through Natural Tunnel in Virginia. The tracks were laid without digging or blasting. *Far right:* a rock formation inside Carlsbad Caverns in New Mexico.

Tunnels in Nature

The outdoor world supplies many examples of tunnels made without human help. Underground streams have worn away passages in many parts of the world to form **caverns**.

Natural **caves** were one of the earliest forms of human shelter. Mankind's first tunneling efforts were probably attempts to improve cave dwellings. Or early people may have tried to hack out a home in the side of a hill where no cave existed before.

Earthworms and many kinds of insects chew or work their way through tunnel-like passages in the earth. They may even chew through wood. The teredo worm, or shipworm, chews tunnels with its tiny, sharp teeth. It burrows into wood in the hulls of ships or on piers that are submerged in water.

An ant colony is really a series of tunnels that may widen in places to form chambers. And the bark beetle spreads the Dutch elm disease fungus as it tunnels underneath the bark of a tree.

Various mammals—moles, rabbits, prairie dogs, and chipmunks—use their sharp claws to dig tunnels to find and store food and to make shelters and hiding places. Woodchucks and groundhogs may dig as far as 20 to 40 feet (6 to 12 m) underground.

The caves found in nature or the tunnels made by animals probably gave early people the idea to dig their own tunnels.

This trail shows the path of an underground tunnel made by a mole. Sometimes other animals—snakes, for example—take over tunnels that were once the homes of burrowing animals.

Parts of a Tunnel

The parts of a tunnel have special names.

The openings to a tunnel are called **portals** or **adits**. Sometimes the entrance is called the **mouth**. The sides are called **sidewalls**. The top is called the **crown** or **roof**. The bottom or floor of the tunnel is known as the **invert**.

The path that a tunnel takes on one level is called the **line**. The path that a tunnel takes upward or downward is called the **grade**.

If the opening of the tunnel goes straight down or at a steep angle into the earth, it is called a **shaft**. Where two tunnel passages run parallel to each other, they are sometimes joined by a short, crosscut tunnel called a **drift**.

A modern tunnel entrance in Albany, New York. Two lanes of tunnels take automobile traffic under the Empire State Plaza, a complex that contains many government buildings.

The **heading** is the part of the tunnel that is being extended or dug out. The wall of rock where digging is taking place is called the **face**. Any rock, earth, or mud removed when a tunnel is being built is called **muck**. A solid block of earth or rock left in place to support the roof is called a **pillar**.

The supports that hold up the roof and walls of a tunnel are called **timbering**, even though today other materials are used instead of the wooden timbers of early mines and tunnels. Braces called **ribs** or steel plates are bolted together. **Roof bolts** are giant screws that are often put into tunnels built through rock to help make them more solid.

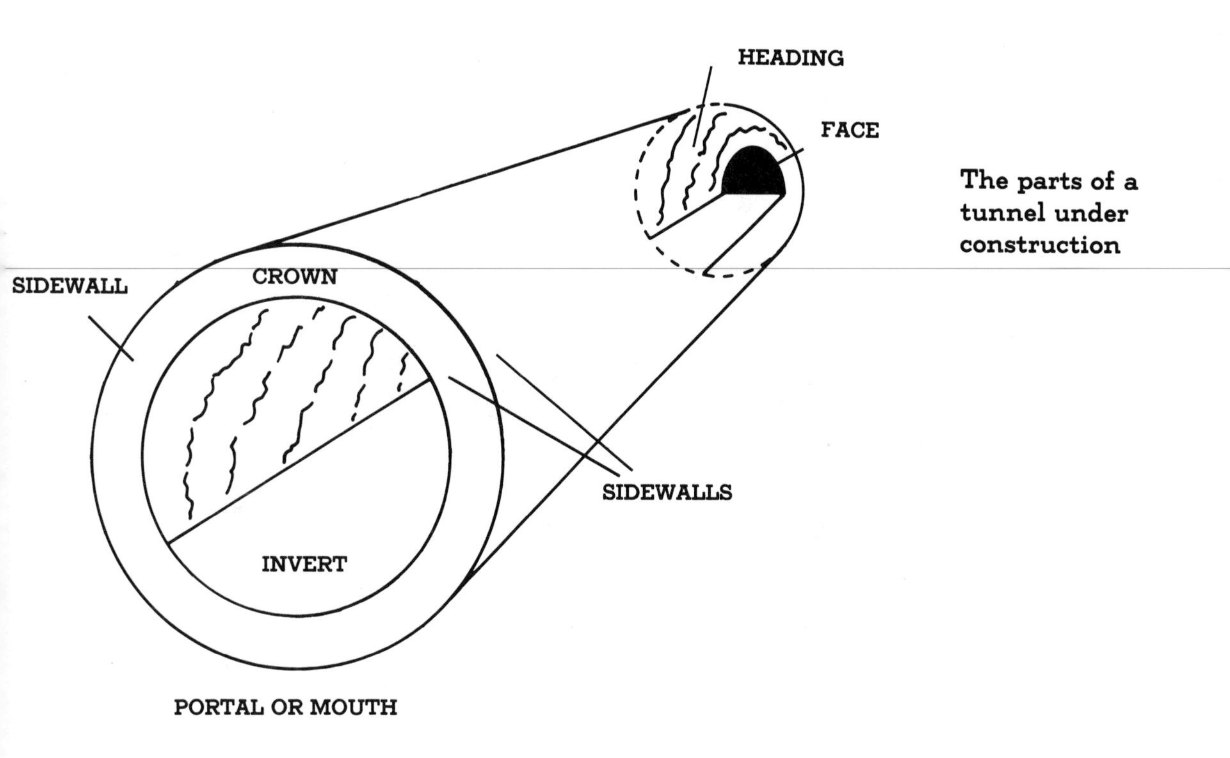

The parts of a tunnel under construction

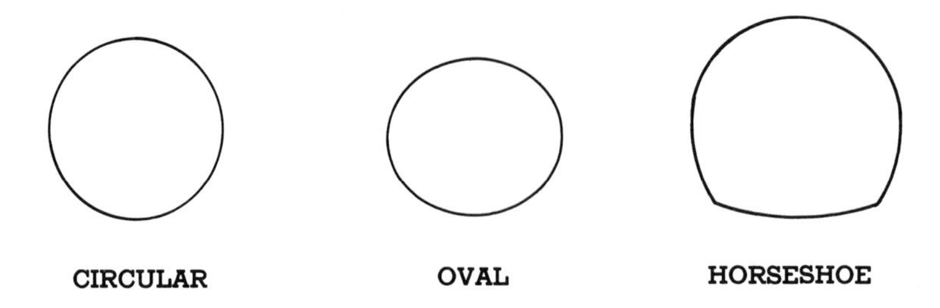

Kinds of Tunnels

Most tunnels are circular or nearly circular in cross section. Circular or oval tunnels usually go through soft ground or under a body of water. Other tunnels may have a flat bottom and walls that are either curved or flat. But the top of a tunnel is almost always rounded, because the arched shape is stronger.

A **horseshoe tunnel** is almost round. A **vertical sidewall tunnel** has a flat bottom surface and straight walls but a top that is rounded. A **basket-handle tunnel** has a flat floor but a top that forms a long, wide arch, or **vault**.

A few tunnels have been made that are square or rectangular, but these shapes are not the best for supporting the weight of rock and soil above. A transportation tunnel may have a flat ceiling that makes it look rectangular but this is not really the roof of the tunnel.

Tunnels are described as **shallow, low-level,** and **high-level**. A shallow tunnel is only a few

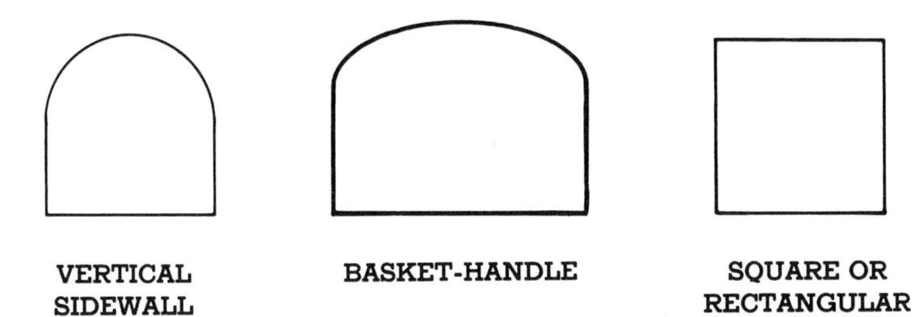

feet below the ground. A low-level tunnel is far under the ground. A high-level tunnel is dug from the surface of the ground through a hill or mountain.

Wind Tunnels

Wind tunnels are special tunnels that are built above the ground. They can vary in size from a tube a few inches in diameter to a tunnel the size of a vast building. The wind in a wind tunnel can be made by large fans or by compressed air or vacuum devices.

Wind tunnels allow scientists to study the effects of wind on airplanes, spacecraft, automobiles, and other vehicles. Here, an F-16XL prototype model is tested in the NASA Langley Research Center, in Virginia.

Before work begins, tunnel designers consider the type of tunnel they need to build, the best shape for it, and the shortest route for it.

Planning and Building a Tunnel

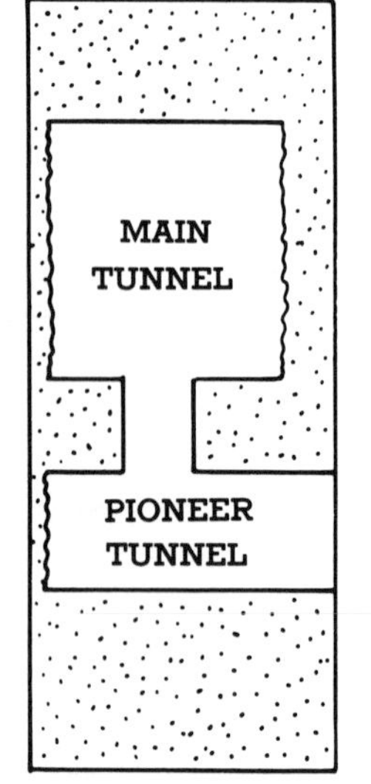

The pioneer tunnel is driven first. Rock will be removed to make one large tunnel opening.

The engineers who plan a tunnel examine the rock and soil where the tunnel is going to be built. Geologists study samples of soil and rock drilled from the site. The designers who plan the tunnel consider everything that will enable them to build a safe, dry, level, and usable tunnel.

Sometimes work proceeds on several sections of a tunnel at the same time. Workers start by digging a narrow **pioneer tunnel**. This is then widened into the main tunnel passage.

In one method two narrow tunnels are advanced side by side. The outer walls of the tunnel are finished and then the center wall separating the two sections is cut away to make one large tunnel.

Sometimes the tunnel begins with one or more deep shafts that go straight down. Then the tunnel builders dig outward from each shaft in two directions. As the sections connect, they form a single tunnel.

Some tunnels are started at each end and workers dig toward each other. When this is done underground or through the center of a mountain, measurements have to be exact so that the different parts of the tunnel will actually meet and line up.

There are several basic methods of building tunnels. In the **cut-and-cover** method, a trench is dug from the surface. Then a tunnel is built inside the trench and is covered over.

True tunnels are called **driven tunnels**. They are made without removing the surface of the ground. There are two kinds of true tunnels that are made by boring through solid rock or soft ground. **Rock tunnels** and **earth tunnels** leave the surface of the ground undisturbed.

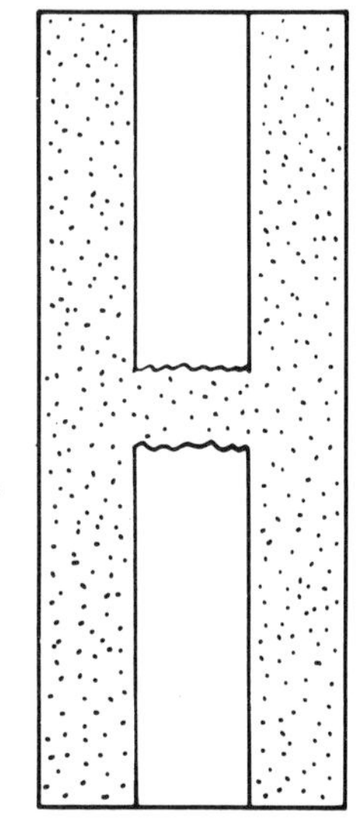

Looking down. When the last small section of rock is dug away, the two sections will join to make one tunnel.

Left: **the cut-and-cover method is used for Pittsburgh's new subway system. The cylinder in the center is a ventilation shaft.** ***Right:*** **the entrance to a mile-long tunnel in Zion National Park, Utah. The tunnel was cut through solid rock.**

Modern equipment makes tunneling safer and easier. Here a crew looks on as a mole crashes through the last section of Rhodes Tunnel in Utah.

Rock Tunneling

One of the hardest tasks workers face is tunneling through rock. A tunnel through rock advances very slowly. Holes are drilled in rings, one inside the other. The holes are then filled with dynamite or other explosives. The rock is blasted into chunks.

A jumbo can be mounted on tracks or a truck.

After blasting, loose rock is scraped away from the sides to prevent cave-ins. Trucks or conveyor belts haul away the debris, or muck.

A **jumbo** is a big machine that has tiers of working platforms mounted on a car that runs on a railroad track. Automatic drills, or **drifters**, mounted on the jumbo attack different parts of the rock face all at the same time. After the drilling, the jumbo can be rolled away. Then the face can be blasted.

A mole is a big machine that has a number of cutting heads with steel teeth that dig into the rock. The tunnel can advance without blasting.

The new heading is then braced or timbered with steel beams or ribs. If the rock is stable enough, it may not need to be braced. Finally, the tunnel will be lined with reinforced concrete.

A giant mole. The head has 27 cutter discs that chip the rock.

Earth Tunneling

The most difficult part of earth tunneling is bracing the soft earth against cave-ins. The invention of the **shield** was the major advance in earth tunneling. A shield is an airtight metal cylinder that is the same size across as the tunnel.

Pumps force air under pressure into the shield.

Land must be graded and roads built at the ends of tunnels. Here a grader prepares the bank in order for cars to be able to drive through a tunnel.

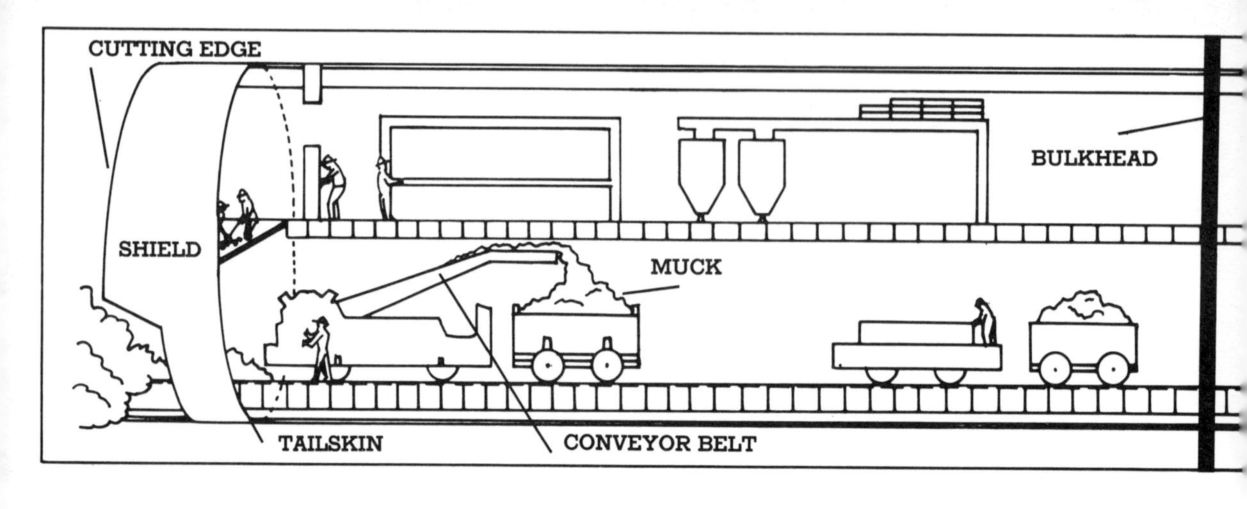

Cutaway view of a tunnel being advanced with a shield.

Left: an air lock chamber, used in the construction of the Holland Tunnel under New York City's Hudson River. *Right:* a shovel operated by compressed air removes muck from the river section of the Lincoln Tunnel, also under the Hudson.

This **compressed air** keeps water out of the tunnel. Workers enter and leave the shield through an **air lock**. This is a steel cylinder with doors at each end. After working in the compressed air compartment, workers must return to the normal atmosphere slowly to prevent gas bubbles from forming in their blood. This serious condition is called the **bends**.

The shield often has a very hard, sharp cutting edge at its forward end. Powerful **jacks** drive the cutting edge forward. Sometimes the front end is a framework called the **diaphragm**. It is sealed off by a strong partition with a number of gates. In

Left: a portal ring is placed in position during the building of the Lincoln Tunnel. *Right:* the finished steel rings form the framework of the Holland Tunnel. Steel takes the place of the wooden timbering used in early tunnels.

soft mud, one or more gates on the front of the shield are opened. The shield moves forward and ribbons of mud ooze backward, like toothpaste squeezed from a tube. The mud is sliced by wires and hauled away. In more solid earth, workmen excavate the material in front of the diaphragm with mechanical **shovels** and **scrapers**. Areas of rock or boulders may need to be blasted.

The open back end of the shield is called the **tailskin**. Muck is carried away through this opening. The tunnel lining of steel plates or concrete or masonry is put in place as the shield moves forward.

Tunnel construction actually takes place within the shield. After each advance of the shield, pieces of a strong metal lining ring are bolted into place to reinforce the tunnel. When the steel ring is in place, it is lined with reinforced concrete or other material. Cement may be pumped through holes in the rings to make a strong wall several inches thick.

The BART (Bay Area Rapid Transit) tunnel for the San Francisco subway system is the world's longest immersed-tube tunnel. It is also the one built in the deepest waters.

Tunnels Under Water

Tunnels that pass underneath rivers or other bodies of water are the most difficult to build since they involve special problems.

Marc Isambard Brunel (1769–1849) of Great Britain invented the shield used for underwater tunneling. The first shield was a rectangular wooden frame with openings through which workers could dig. **Jacks** powered by large screws that were turned forced the shield forward. Later the one-piece cylindrical metal shield replaced this machine.

Shields filled with compressed air are now always used for building underwater tunnels. A **bulkhead**, or airtight wall, seals off the end of the tunnel behind the shield. Work is completed while compressed air keeps water from

Left: a roadbed of rock in place in the Holland Tunnel. Pavement will be laid on top of this rock. *Right:* workers in the Lincoln Tunnel rivet a section of the steel ring. People who work in earth or underwater tunnels are sometimes called sandhogs.

flooding the tunnel. The air pressure is changed according to the depth of the tunnel and the nature of the ground being tunneled through.

Some underwater tunnels are built by the cut-and-cover method. A trench is prepared across the bed of the river or other body of water. Barges float finished tunnel sections into place. The pre-made tunnel sections are sunk into place and fastened together. The tunnel and trench are then covered over. This is often called the **immersed-tube** or **submerged-tube** method for building underwater tunnels.

Making a Tunnel Usable

After a tunnel has been built, a roadway or railroad track may be laid to run through it. This is usually built in a boxlike enclosure that sits

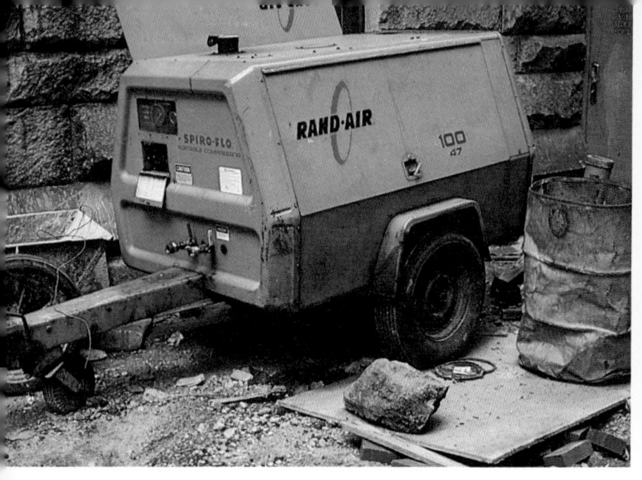

Left: compressed air, forced into a tunnel by a machine like this one, keeps water out and the inside dry. *Right:* air shafts, fan systems, and air pumps bring in fresh air and pump out stale air.

inside the actual tunnel. The walls may be painted or covered with tiles.

All tunnel designers must see that the tunnel stays dry and that it has enough fresh air and enough light.

A tunnel must have a steady supply of fresh air. During construction, a tunnel can fill up with hot air, smoke, dust, and gases. Sometimes this can cause an explosion. Tunnel builders often dig into underground streams or pockets of mud. Powerful suction pumps carry water and steam away and prevent the tunnel from filling up. Watertight concrete linings and drainage pumps keep the tunnel dry after it is finished.

Workers who build tunnels use battery lights and temporary electric lines. After the tunnel is completed (right), permanent electric lights are installed.

Tunnels Through the Ages

Many ancient peoples dug out underground chambers for their tombs and temples. The ancient Egyptians built tombs that could be reached by tunnel entrances. Around 2180 B.C. the Babylonians built a tunnel under the Euphrates River. It was a large brick tube built in the riverbed while the water was low. It was then covered over, and the river was allowed to follow its course. This tunnel was more than a half mile long and linked the royal palace and temple.

In ancient Israel, a tunnel built around 700 B.C. carried water right through the walls of the city of Jerusalem. In ancient Persia and in other parts of the Middle East, tunnels called **kanats** were dug through solid rock. They led to underground reservoirs.

The catacombs were tunnels built underneath Rome in ancient times. They were burial places for the dead as well as hiding places for people fleeing persecutors.

The Romans built tunnels for drainage purposes. One huge tunnel emptied the water from a lake near Rome. The Romans also dug short tunnels for military reasons. This was a use for tunnels that was continued into the Middle Ages. Tunnels were used to undermine the walls of a city during a siege. And people under attack often made daring escapes through secret tunnel passages.

The modern age of tunnel building began around 1760. Many tunnels constructed between 1760 and 1830 let canals pass through hills, mountains, and other natural obstacles.

The first tunnel in the United States was built in 1818 on the Schuylkill Navigational Canal near Philadelphia, Pennsylvania. The Union Canal Tunnel was dug between 1825 and 1927 near Lebanon, Pennsylvania. It is 720 feet (218 m) long.

In the late 1800s, scientists and engineers began to realize the possibilities for tunneling

The Thames Tunnel was opened in 1843. It took eighteen years to build and connected the two sides of the Thames River in London.

through mountains, under rivers and cities, and for expanding railroad transportation systems. The Hoosac Tunnel, built from 1852 to 1873, was America's longest railroad tunnel until the Moffat Tunnel was completed in 1928.

The success of railroad tunnels in the United States and Great Britain inspired the underground railway, or subway, systems. Subways make rapid travel possible underneath the busy streets of crowded cities.

Cities in the United States and Europe began to build subway systems in the last half of the nineteenth century. In 1863 the first segment of London's underground system, or tube, was begun. Paris, Boston, New York, Moscow, and other cities soon built subways of their own.

Left: **the Hoosac Tunnel in western Massachusetts was America's first important railroad tunnel. It is almost 5 miles (8 km) long.** ***Right:*** **the Moffat Tunnel in Colorado extends over 6 miles (9.6 km) under the Continental Divide.**

Left: **a tunnel in London's Underground system.** ***Right:*** **the cut-and-cover method is much like constructing a building in a trench. Subway tunnels and platforms are built from steel framework and poured concrete.**

Alpine Tunnels

The Alpine tunnels were one of the most important engineering projects planned in the nineteenth century. The Alps are a high mountain range more than 500 miles (800 km) long. They separate Italy from the rest of Europe and since ancient times have made travel difficult.

The Mont Cenis Tunnel, linking France and Italy, opened in 1871 and was the first great tunnel in the Alps. The tunnel is sometimes known as Fréjus. At $8\frac{1}{2}$ miles (13.6 km) long, it was the first tunnel dug with compressed air drills.

The Simplon Tunnel is one of the world's longest railroad tunnels. It is $12\frac{1}{3}$ miles (19.8 km) long and crosses the border between Switzerland and Italy.

The Loetschberg and Mont Blanc Tunnels are the two major Alpine tunneling projects planned and completed in the twentieth century.

Left: The St. Gotthard Tunnel, more than 9 miles (14.5 km) long, is one of the longest tunnels in the Alps. *Right:* the Mont Blanc Tunnel connects Italy and France. It is 7.2 miles (11.6 km) long—one of the world's longest automobile tunnels.

Modern Tunnels in the United States

Some of the major tunneling projects of this century have been the tunnels that link Manhattan Island with the areas that surround the heart of New York City.

In 1927 the Holland Tunnel under the Hudson River was opened. It was the first automobile tunnel to connect New York City with New Jersey. It was named not after the Netherlands, but after the chief engineer.

In 1950 the Brooklyn Battery Tunnel was completed. It connects Manhattan with Brooklyn.

The United States' most recent large tunnel project has been the 23-mile (37 km)-long Chesapeake Bay Bridge Tunnel that spans the mouth of Chesapeake Bay. Over 17 miles (27.4 km) of the project are underwater tunnel sections.

Opened in 1937, the Lincoln Tunnel is the only three-tube vehicular tunnel in the world. *Left:* the highway approach on the New Jersey side of the Hudson River. *Right:* modern equipment scrubs tunnel walls.

Tunneling into the Future

Tunnel building is a lively branch of engineering. Many new building methods that make use of the latest advances in science are being developed. Scientists are finding ways to use nuclear energy and the high-powered beams of light called **lasers** to cut through rock quickly and easily. Longer and deeper tunnels are being planned every day.

Some of the major challenges of this century are long tunnels being built under parts of the sea. The Seikan Tunnel is now being built to connect the city of Honshu in Japan with the island of Hokkaido. It passes under the Tsugaru Channel at a maximum depth of 780 feet (234 m).

Lasers are used to make sure the walls are straight and level during construction of a water supply tunnel in California.

Other major undersea tunnels between Alaska and Siberia or under the Strait of Gibraltar that would connect Europe with Africa have been discussed. Scientists could build these challenging tunnels even today, but it may be years before international cooperation makes them possible.

People dream of a day in the future when tunnels thousands of miles long will be cut through the earth between distant cities. These tunnels would allow frictionless trains going at tremendous speeds to travel between cities in a matter of minutes. Rapid transit systems could make commuters of people who work thousands of miles from their homes! But such plans are still a long way off—perhaps a hundred years or more.

Left: **one of tomorrow's possible tunnels was begun over a hundred years ago but then abandoned. Called the Chunnel, it may some day run under the English Channel and connect England with France.** ***Right:*** **workers on the long Seikan Tunnel. Due to be finished in 1986, the tunnel's total length will be 33½ miles (53.8 km).**

Words About Tunnels

Adit. An opening to a tunnel. Also known as a portal or mouth.

Air lock. A sealed chamber at the end of a shield. This space allows an underground worker to return gradually to normal atmosphere.

Aqueduct. A tunnel that carries water.

Basket-handle tunnel. A tunnel that has a flat floor but an arched, or vaulted, top.

Bends. A sickness caused when air bubbles form in a person's blood. It can happen when a tunnel worker does not return to normal atmosphere slowly.

Bulkhead. An airtight wall built across an underwater tunnel.

Compressed air. Air under pressure. It provides tunnel builders with a safe atmosphere in which to work underground.

Crown. The roof or top of a tunnel.

Cut-and-cover method. A way of building tunnels. A trench is dug from the surface and is then covered over.

Diaphragm. A framework at the front end of a shield.

Drift. A short, cross tunnel that sometimes joins two other parallel tunnel passages.

Drifter. An automatic drill that digs out rock for tunnels.

Driven tunnel. A tunnel that is made without removing the surface of the ground.

Earth tunnel. A kind of driven tunnel that is made by boring through soft ground.

Face. The wall of rock where tunnel digging takes place.

Grade. The upward or downward slope of a tunnel.

Heading. The part of a tunnel that is being dug out.

High-level tunnel. A tunnel that is dug from the surface of the ground through a mountain.

Horseshoe tunnel. A tunnel that is almost round.

Immersed-tube method. A way of building tunnels underwater in which pre-made sections are floated into place. Also called submerged-tube method.

Invert. The bottom or floor of a tunnel.

Jumbo. A big drilling machine with several tiers of drilling platforms.

Laser. A high-powered light beam that can easily cut through rock.

Low-level tunnel. A tunnel that is far underground.

Mole. A machine that has a number of cutting heads with steel teeth that cut into rock.

Mouth. A name for the opening of a tunnel.

Muck. Any rock, earth, or mud that is removed when a tunnel is being built.

Pioneer tunnel. A small tunnel that is then expanded into a larger one.

Portal. The opening to a tunnel. Sometimes called an adit or mouth.

Rock tunnel. A tunnel made by drilling through rock.

Roof bolts. Giant screws that are put into tunnels built through rock. They help keep rock from falling down.

Sandhogs. Underground workers who build tunnels.

Scraper. A machine used in tunnel building to excavate rock.

Shaft. A tunnel opening that goes steeply down into the earth.

Shield. An airtight metal cylinder for tunneling through earth or underwater.

Sidewall. The side walls of a tunnel.

Tailskin. The open back end of a shield.

Timbering. Wooden or metal braces or supports that hold up the roof and walls of a tunnel.

Vault. A long, wide arched top of a tunnel.

Vertical sidewall tunnel. A tunnel with a flat bottom and straight walls but a rounded top.

Index